Spiritual Bootcamp

Spiritual Bootcamp

by
John MacArthur, Jr.

"GRACE TO YOU"
P.O. Box 4000
Panorama City, CA   91412

© 1990 by
JOHN F. MACARTHUR, JR.

ISBN: 0-8024-5324-4

1 2 3 4 5 6 Printing/LC/Year 94 93 92 91 90

Printed in the United States of America

Contents

These Bible studies are taken from messages delivered by Pastor-Teacher John MacArthur, Jr., at Grace Community Church in Panorama City, California. These messages have been combined into a 4-tape album titled *Spiritual Bootcamp*. You may purchase this series either in an attractive vinyl cassette album or as individual cassettes. To purchase these tapes, request the album *Spiritual Bootcamp*, or ask for the tapes by their individual GC numbers. Please consult the current price list; then, send your order, making your check payable to:

The Master's Communication
P.O. Box 4000
Panorama City, CA 91412

Or call the following toll-free number:
1-800-55-GRACE

1
How to Study Scripture

Outline

Introduction
A. The Authority of God's Word
B. The Priority of God's Word

Lesson
I. The Necessity of Bible Study
  A. For Spiritual Growth
  B. For Spiritual Victory
  C. For Spiritual Service
  D. For Spiritual Blessing
  E. For Spiritual Counseling
II. The Process of Bible Study
  A. The Preparation
  B. The Procedure
    1. Read the Bible
      a) Short New Testament books
      b) Long New Testament books
      c) Old Testament books
    2. Study the Bible
      a) Topical studies
      b) Biographical studies
      c) Study tools
        (1) Concordances
        (2) Topical indexes
        (3) Commentaries
    3. Teach the Bible
    4. Follow a godly example
    5. Hear the Bible taught

Questions and Answers

Introduction

A. The Authority of God's Word

Christians understand that the Bible is God's revelation—His authoritative standard for life. Other sources of information may help us through life, but only the Bible has divine authority. Therefore we must be diligent students of the Word, faithfully reading it to discover what it says and systematically studying it to learn what it means.

B. The Priority of God's Word

Because we are blessed with many books, tapes, and other biblical resources, it is possible to study about the Bible while neglecting the Bible itself. As helpful as such resources might be, they are no substitute for God's Word and the spiritual nourishment it brings.

Lesson

I. THE NECESSITY OF BIBLE STUDY

A. For Spiritual Growth

1. 1 Peter 2:2—"As newborn babes, desire the pure milk of the word, that ye may grow by it."

   Peter's analogy of a baby illustrates the importance of God's Word to spiritual growth. If a baby is deprived of nourishment, it will eventually die. If a Christian doesn't feed on the Word, he or she will languish spiritually and be of little use to the kingdom of God.

   In addition, the New Testament refers to Christians as being born again (John 3:7; 1 Pet. 1:3), children of God (Rom. 8:16; 1 John 3:1), and adopted sons (Rom. 8:14; Eph. 1:5). Those terms imply that all believers have the capacity for spiritual growth. Peter even commands us to grow (2 Pet. 3:18).

2. 1 Corinthians 3:1-2—The apostle Paul said, "I, brethren, could not speak unto you as unto spiritual, but as unto carnal, even as unto babes in Christ. I have fed you with milk, and not with solid food; for to this time ye were not able to bear it, neither yet now are ye able."

Paul understood the need to feed believers with God's Word, and he used the metaphors of milk and meat to describe simple and complex biblical truths. That doesn't mean that parts of Scripture are milk and parts are meat. All Scripture is either milk or meat, depending on how deeply you go into the text. The simple truth that "God so loved the world" (John 3:16) might be a "milk" statement to a new believer, but the same statement may be meat to one who has learned the deeper truths of God's love as revealed in Scripture.

3. Colossians 2:6-7—"As ye have . . . received Christ Jesus the Lord, so walk ye in him, rooted and built up in him, and established in the faith."

"The faith" in this context refers to the content of Christianity—the doctrines of Scripture. Increased understanding of Scripture brings increased steadfastness in Christ.

4. Jeremiah 15:16—The prophet Jeremiah said to the Lord, "Thy words were found, and I did eat them, and thy word was unto me the joy and rejoicing of mine heart." Jeremiah received God's Word with such enthusiasm that it was like dining to him. It was his spiritual food and sustenance, and it brought him great joy.

5. Acts 20:32—Paul said to the Ephesian elders, "I commend you to God, and to the word of his grace, which is able to build you up, and to give you an inheritance among all them who are sanctified."

Our usefulness to Christ is directly related to our spiritual maturity, which is related to our knowledge of God's Word. That's why Bible study is so important.

B. For Spiritual Victory

The way to defeat sin is to know and apply the Word.

1. Ephesians 6:13, 17—"Take unto you the whole armor of God, that ye may be able to withstand in the evil day, and having done all, to stand. . . . And take . . . the sword of the Spirit, which is the word of God."

The armor of God is our protection against Satan's attacks. Every piece of armor listed in Ephesians 6:14-17 is a defensive weapon except the sword of the Spirit, our only offensive weapon.

2. Psalm 119:11—The psalmist said to the Lord, "Thy word have I hidden in mine heart, that I might not sin against thee."

3. Psalm 119:9—"[How] shall a young man cleanse his way? By taking heed thereto according to thy word." Godliness results from living according to God's Word.

How Are You Programming Your Spiritual Computer?

Conditioning your mind is similar to programming a computer. Perhaps you've heard the term G.I.G.O.: "Garbage In, Garbage Out." What goes into a computer determines the output. Similarly, whatever you program into your mind will eventually come out in your speech and behavior. As you learn the principles of God's Word and meditate on them, they begin to dominate your thinking and govern your behavior. That produces righteousness and holiness.

Are you programming your mind with God's Word?

4. 1 John 2:14—The apostle John said, "I have written unto you, young men, because ye are strong, and the word of God abideth in you, and ye have overcome the wicked one." Spiritual strength and victory are the result of God's Word abiding within you.

C. For Spiritual Service

A thorough knowledge of Scripture is crucial for anyone preparing for spiritual service. Otherwise he or she might unwittingly participate in activities that violate God's principles.

1. Joshua 1:8-9—The Lord said to Joshua, "This book of the law shall not depart out of thy mouth, but thou shalt meditate therein day and night, that thou mayest observe to do according to all that is written therein; for then thou shalt make thy way prosperous, and then thou shalt have good success. Have not I commanded thee? Be strong and of good courage; be not afraid, neither be thou dismayed; for the Lord thy God is with thee wherever thou goest."

True success comes from knowing and applying God's Word. As Moses' successor, Joshua had a tremendous task ahead of him. He was to lead the Israelites into the Promised Land. God assured Him that if he would meditate on His Word he would receive the strength, instruction, and comfort he needed for the task.

2. 1 Timothy 4:6—Paul said to Timothy, "If thou put the brethren in remembrance of [the things I have said], thou shalt be a good minister of Jesus Christ, nourished up in the words of faith and of good doctrine."

The Greek word translated "minister" describes a servant, one who administrates the goods and property of another. A good minister is one who administrates biblical truth.

D. For Spiritual Blessing

When the Bible speaks of man's being blessed, it most often refers to the reception of some temporal or spiritual benefit (*Evangelical Dictionary of Theology*, Walter A. Elwell, ed. [Grand Rapids: Baker, 1984], p. 162). Implied in a blessing is the sense of well-being and happiness that comes from knowing that God is at work on our behalf.

The Bible is a source of blessing. The more we study the Word, the happier we will be, regardless of our circumstances. That's a practical principle to know, especially if you're unhappy or in the midst of difficult circumstances. Psalm 1:1-2 says, "Blessed is the man who walketh not in the counsel of the ungodly, nor standeth in the way of sinners, nor sitteth in the seat of the scornful. But his delight is in the law of the Lord; and in his law doth he meditate day and night."

E. For Spiritual Counseling

When people are in trouble, the best way to help them is to show them God's solution to their problems. Then help them apply that solution to their lives. That requires a thorough knowledge of biblical principles.

1. 2 Timothy 2:2—Paul said to Timothy, "The things that thou hast heard from me among many witnesses, the same commit thou to faithful men, who shall be able to teach others also." That's the process of discipleship. But before we can teach others, we must learn the principles ourselves.

2. 1 Peter 3:15—"Sanctify the Lord God in your hearts, and be ready always to give an answer to every man that asketh you a reason of the hope that is in you, with meekness and fear." We must know what we believe and why we believe it so that we can give an appropriate response to those who ask about our faith.

II. THE PROCESS OF BIBLE STUDY

A. The Preparation

Peter said to lay "aside all malice, and all guile, and hypocrisies, and envies, and all evil speakings" before studying the Word (1 Pet. 2:1).

Sin is the greatest hindrance to effective Bible study. Therefore we must never approach God's Word until our hearts and minds have been purified through prayer and confession. James 1:21 says, "Put away all filthiness and overflow-

12

ing of wickedness, and receive with meekness the engrafted word, which is able to save your souls."

B. The Procedure

1. Read the Bible

God promises to bless those who read His Word. Revelation 1:3 says, "Blessed is he that readeth, and they that hear the words of this prophecy, and keep those things which are written in it."

Paul said to Timothy, "Till I come, give attendance to reading [of Scripture]" (1 Tim. 4:13). Reading Scripture is a priority we need to maintain on a daily basis.

I used to struggle with reading the Bible because I easily forgot what I had read. I soon realized that reading Scripture repetitiously was the best way for me to remember it—this excerpt from Isaiah being my inspiration: "precept upon precept, precept upon precept; line upon line, line upon line; here a little, and there a little" (Isa. 28:13).

a) Short New Testament books

Start with a short book like 1 John, and read it once a day for thirty days from a Bible translation you are familiar with (I recommend the *New American Standard*, King James, or *New International Version*). After thirty days, you will know the content of 1 John so well that you'll be able to visualize the location of various passages on their respective pages. Forming mental pictures is part of the learning process.

Repetitious reading will not always tell you the meaning of Scripture, but it is a great way to learn what it says, and that's the first step of interpretation. Additionally, as you continue to read the same book over and over, your ability to observe the events, people, and principles in it is heightened.

b) Long New Testament books

Longer books should be broken into segments for repetitious reading. For example, the gospel of John contains twenty-one chapters. You can read chapters 1-7 for thirty days, then chapters 8-14, then chapters 15-21. In ninety days you will have read John's gospel thirty times. In two and a half years you can read the entire New Testament thirty times!

c) Old Testament books

That approach isn't as practical for the Old Testament. I suggest reading it all the way through and then going back and starting again as a lifetime practice. Most of the Old Testament is historical narrative, which lends itself to that approach.

There are many benefits to reading the Bible systematically. For one thing, as you progress in your Bible reading, your ability to cross-reference will increase. A topic, principle, or word in one passage will trigger your memory about another passage that discusses the same thing. That will give you a more thorough grasp of biblical teaching on any given subject and will make you less dependent on concordances and other reference tools.

When I want to explain a passage of Scripture, I usually go to other passages that shed light on it. That's the starting point for interpretation, because Scripture is the best interpreter of Scripture. It never contradicts itself, and it often repeats the same principle in a different set of circumstances. If you read Scripture repeatedly, listen to Bible teaching at church, and attend Bible studies, you will have a good idea of how to interpret the Bible.

2. Study the Bible

a) Topical studies

Topical studies help us learn what the Bible teaches about any given topic by tracing it throughout Scripture. For example, the prayers of the Bible make a great topical study. You could start in Genesis and identify every passage in which someone prays. Note who prays, what he or she says, and how the prayer is answered. You could limit your study to the prayers of Paul. Be sure to apply what you learn to your own prayers.

You can use a topical index to locate every passage in which forgiveness or any other biblical topic is discussed. After reading each reference, you will have a good idea of what the Bible says about that topic.

b) Biographical studies

Biographical studies help us learn what the Bible teaches about various people by tracing their lives through Scripture.

You may want to study the lives of Old Testament men such as Elijah, David, and Joseph, or New Testament men such as Peter, Paul, and Andrew. We can learn much from each person's life-style, character traits, and relationship to God.

c) Study tools

We have noted that study tools such as books and tapes should never replace our time in God's Word, but they do play an important role nonetheless. You should find good resources to help you in your studies. Concentrate on reference books that you will use again and again. Popular Christian books about someone's testimony or experience can be helpful and encouraging, but Bible study requires reference works.

(1) Concordances

A concordance gives an alphabetical listing of biblical words and their references. An exhaustive concordance also includes other helpful information such as Hebrew and Greek dictionaries. Examples of good concordances are Strong's *Exhaustive Concordance of the Bible*, Young's *Analytical Concordance to the Holy Bible*, Cruden's *Complete*

Concordance of the Old and New Testaments, and the *New American Standard Exhaustive Concordance of the Bible.*

(2) Topical indexes

Topical indexes list major biblical themes alphabetically along with the primary references for each theme. Harold Monser's *Topical Index and Digest of the Bible* and Nave's *Topical Bible* are two examples of topical indexes.

(3) Commentaries

Commentaries explain the meaning of Scripture. The one-volume *Wycliffe Bible Commentary* is a good place for new Christians to start because it gives a brief explanation of every passage of Scripture. We also have *The MacArthur New Testament Commentary* for those who desire a more in-depth study of Scripture.

3. Teach the Bible

Teaching others what you have learned from Scripture is as important as Bible study itself. It's our responsibility to do so (2 Tim. 2:2), and it's a great source of motivation and accountability. Even if you're a new Christian, others can benefit from what you've learned. The Lord might bring an unbeliever into your life with whom you can share the gospel or a believer who knows more Scripture than you but who may benefit from your fresh insights. Be faithful to take advantage of every opportunity.

4. Follow a godly example

Following a godly example is an important element of applying biblical principles to your life. It may be your pastor or another Christian brother or sister, but it should be someone you can be accountable to.

5. Hear the Bible taught

Listening to good Bible teaching at church and in group Bible studies is a necessary supplement to personal Bible study but should never be a substitute for it. We need both public and private Bible study.

Do You Pursue Biblical Knowledge or Entertainment?

I've seen many new Christians whose only contact with Christianity is going from one Christian entertainment event to another. One week a current Christian "star" is speaking or singing nearby, so they attend there. The next week the latest Christian movie is being shown somewhere else, so they go there. They haven't learned the discipline of submitting to systematic Bible teaching.

What about you? Do you prefer entertainment over biblical instruction?

Questions and Answers

1. *In what order should we read the books of the Bible?*

I do not recommend any particular order, other than perhaps alternating between a short book and a long one. For example, after reading 1 John and the gospel of John, read Philippians, Romans, 1 Timothy, Mark, and Colossians in that order. Often the Holy Spirit will draw you to a book that meets a specific need in your life.

2. *What did you mean when you said that a spiritual babe would languish if it didn't get fed?*

I was speaking in a metaphorical sense. Christians who don't feed on God's Word will forfeit their usefulness, joy, and blessing. They will not forfeit their salvation.

3. *If a professing Christian shows no hunger for the Word, what is his spiritual condition and what can be done for him?*

In John 8:31 Jesus says, "If ye continue in my word, then are ye my disciples indeed." A true disciple is one who continues in God's Word. That presupposes a desire for the Word. If he has no desire, the person may not really be a Christian. He or she needs to undergo the self-examination that 2 Corinthians 13:5 commands.

However, some Christians are in churches where the Bible isn't taught or where they are not encouraged to study the Word, so their desire may be minimal. Others are Christians for many years before they commit themselves to serious study. Still others simply have a tenacity for learning. But all true believers will demonstrate some desire to know and obey God's Word.

We can encourage those whose desire is waning by pointing out the benefits and blessings of Bible study and by holding them accountable.

4. *Would you elaborate on the importance of finding a godly person to pattern one's life after?*

Paul said to Timothy, "Be thou an example [to] the believers, in word, in conduct, in love, in spirit, in faith, in purity" (1 Tim. 4:12). A leader's example will have a profound impact on those he leads because people tend to imitate others. That's why spiritual leaders must be above reproach (1 Tim. 3:2).

Although Christ is the ultimate example, Paul exhorted believers to follow his own example as he followed Christ's (1 Cor. 4:16; 11:1; Phil. 3:17; 2 Thess. 3:9). We need godly people who will set a pattern for us to follow.

5. *Since we all have sin in our lives, isn't there a danger in relying too heavily on human examples?*

It is true that we are all sinful, but it isn't sinless perfection that makes someone a godly example—it's how the person deals with sin. Paul said, "Christ Jesus came into the world to save sinners, of whom I am chief" (1 Tim. 1:15). Paul was aware of his failures, but that didn't deter him from pursuing godliness and serving as an example to others.

You should follow others only to the degree that they follow Christ. Follow a transparent person through whom you see Christ. If you cease to see Christ through him, you must cease following his example. Diotrephes, probably a leader in the early church, loved "to have the pre-eminence" (3 John 9). But Scripture attributes preeminence to Christ alone. Therefore we know that Diotrephes usurped the place of Christ and disqualified himself from being worthy of imitation.

6. *How do we establish a godly habit such as daily Bible study?*

Habits are developed by repeated behavior. The key is to begin a routine of daily Bible reading—preferably when you're young —and it will soon develop into a habit.

Good habits performed for the right reasons are an important part of life. Jesus Himself was in the habit of retreating to the Mount of Olives for prayer (Luke 22:39).

7. *If an individual is involved in a ministry that requires daily Bible study, is it still necessary to have a time of Bible reading over and above that study?*

Not necessarily. All time spent in God's Word is profitable. For example if I study from 9:00 A.M. until 5:00 P.M., I don't feel guilty because I didn't have my "devotions." Devotions or daily Bible reading is one way to develop consistency in God's Word, but more intense study is ideal.

8. *Should people who attend or teach a weekly Bible study augment their study with systematic Bible reading?*

Yes. Daily time in the Word is essential, and you should guard that time carefully.

9. *Please outline the procedure you use to study a passage of Scripture.*

Step one: Read the text. I read it repeatedly in several English versions and in the Greek text. I don't intentionally memorize the passage, but I read it so often that it saturates my mind.

Step two: Identify key concepts. The more I read the passage the clearer its concepts become. I write down everything I discover from the passage. My goal is to learn as much as possible from the passage itself before going to outside sources.

Step three: Formulate an initial outline from the key concepts.

Step four: Study the passage verse by verse. I read as many sources of information on the passage as I can find—perhaps ten or twelve commentaries plus biographical studies and other technical resources.

Step five: Formulate a final outline from all the information you've studied.

10. *What do you do when you don't feel like reading the Bible?*

Recognize that when you don't want to read it is when you need it most. Bible study takes discipline, and that must be cultivated through diligent effort. Even more important, Bible study is a matter of obedience (1 Pet. 2:1-2). Keeping that perspective will help you not to neglect the Word.

I understand the difficulty of maintaining continuity in the Word. Vacations are my toughest times because they break my pattern of study. Sometimes I skip two or three days at a time, and that has a noticeable effect on me. In our human weakness we all struggle with that.

11. *What resources do you recommend for teaching the Bible to children?*

There are several good Bible translations and other helps for children, including:

- *The New International Version*—children's edition.

- *The Living Bible*—the Old Testament is especially good.

- *Leading Little Ones to God*, by Marian Schoolland—a systematic theology for children.

12. *How do you direct a new Christian in choosing a church?*

The best way is to teach the person what the Bible says we should look for in a church. We have some helpful resources:

the tape series and study guides titled *Marks of a Healthy Church* (Moody, 1990) and *The Anatomy of a Church* (Moody, 1986).

Once believers know how to evaluate a church, they can identify the best churches in their geographical area and then follow the leading of the Holy Spirit in selecting one to attend.

13. *Is there a danger in relying too heavily on commentaries and other study helps?*

Yes, but the more common danger is neglecting them. Many people meditate on Scripture without first interpreting it properly. Consequently, they risk meditating on error. Scripture has only one meaning, and accurate interpretation seeks to discover that meaning. The issue isn't what the Bible means to you or me, but what it means—period.

We must read Scripture to determine what it says, study Scripture to determine what it means, and *then* meditate on it to determine how to apply it to our lives. Commentaries and other resources help us to discover the meaning of Scripture so that we can meditate on truth rather than on error, but that should never replace meditation on Scripture itself. Paul said, "Whatever things are true, whatever things are honest, whatever things are just, whatever things are pure, whatever things are lovely, whatever things are of good report; if there be any virtue, and if there be any praise, think on these things" (Phil. 4:8).

Focusing on the Facts

1. Why is Bible study necessary? Give five reasons (see pp. 8-12).
2. What analogy for Scripture did Peter use in 1 Peter 2:2 (see p. 8)?
3. All Scripture is either _____ or _____ , depending on how deeply you go into the text (see p. 9).
4. To what does "the faith" refer in Colossians 2:7 (see p. 9)?
5. What is the only offensive weapon mentioned in the list of the Christian's spiritual armor (Eph. 6:17; see p. 10)?
6. What is God's command and promise to Joshua in Joshua 1:8-9 (see p. 11)?
7. A good minister is one who _____ biblical truth (see p. 11).

8. What does Psalm 1:1-2 say about the godly man (see p. 12)?
9. How should we prepare for Bible study (1 Pet. 2:1-2; James 1:21; see pp. 12-13)?
10. List two benefits of reading Scripture repeatedly (see p. 14).
11. What is a concordance used for? A topical index? A commentary (see pp. 15-16)?

Pondering the Principles

1. Many Christians suffer spiritual defeat because their knowledge of biblical principles isn't what it should be. Is that true of you? Read Matthew 4:1-11. What specific temptations did Satan present to Jesus (vv. 3, 6, 9)? How did Jesus deal with them (vv. 4, 7, 10)? What was the result (v. 11)? Do you have a Bible study plan that will equip you to be victorious in times of temptation? If not, are you willing to develop one today?

2. We have seen that an important element in Bible study is submitting yourself to teaching from the pulpit and in small group studies. Sadly, many Christians haven't cultivated that discipline and have all but abandoned Bible teaching for various forms of "Christian entertainment." Such neglect always has a devastating effect on individual lives and on the corporate life of the church. Are your priorities right? Don't fall prey to choosing superficial entertainment over scriptural enlightenment.

2
How to Pray

Outline

Introduction
A. The Nature of Prayer
    1. It is like breathing
    2. It is talking to God
B. The Abuse of Prayer
    1. Requesting what we don't need
    2. Requesting what we already have
    3. Requesting with vain repetition
C. The Mode of Prayer
D. The Posture for Prayer
E. The Effects of Prayer
    1. It activates God's power
    2. It aligns us with God's will

Lesson
I. The Necessity of Prayer
    A. It Is Commanded
        1. We are to be watchful
        2. We are to be faithful
    B. It Glorifies God
    C. It Brings Blessing
    D. It Brings Results
        1. The fact of its results
        2. The timing of its results
        3. The nature of its results
II. The Conditions of Prayer
    A. Praying in Jesus' Name
        1. Explained
        2. Illustrated
        3. Applied

Introduction

A. The Nature of Prayer

    1. It is like breathing

        Praying is to the spiritual life what breathing is to the physical life. At birth we enter into an atmosphere that immediately exerts pressure on our lungs. That forces us to take air in and to begin to breathe. That's why it's more difficult to hold your breath than it is to breathe.

        Similarly, when you're born into the family of God, you enter into a spiritual atmosphere wherein God's presence and grace exert pressure, or influence, on your life. Prayer is the normal response to that pressure.

    2. It is talking to God

        Communication is an undeniable part of life. That's why most parents eagerly await a child's first word and then spend countless hours teaching that child to communicate. It's the same with Christians, who desire to respond to God's presence and grace by communicating with Him. And He delights in their prayers (Prov. 15:8).

The level of some people's communication with God is little poems such as "Now I Lay Me Down to Sleep." Others use eloquent words, deep theological truths, and lots of "thees" and "thous." Neither of those extremes is wrong when offered from a pure heart, but the essence of prayer is talking to God as you would to a beloved friend—without pretense or flippancy.

Scripture is God's communication to us. Prayer is our communication to Him. Apart from the Word, prayer is a one-sided conversation. That's why it's important to study Scripture.

You can pray to any member of the Trinity—Father, Son, or Holy Spirit. You can even direct your prayer to all three, if you wish. That's perfectly acceptable.

B. The Abuse of Prayer

Christians often abuse prayer in several ways.

1. Requesting what we don't need

Sometimes we ask God for things we don't need or shouldn't have (cf. James 4:3). Fortunately, He doesn't always give us what we ask for.

2. Requesting what we already have

Sometimes we ask God for peace, but we already have the peace that passes understanding (Phil. 4:7). Or we request grace, but we already have grace that is sufficient for every situation (2 Cor. 12:9). Or we pray for love, but God's love has already been "shed abroad in our hearts by the Holy Spirit" (Rom. 5:5).

James says we ought to ask for wisdom (James 1:5). That will help us to know what is already ours in Christ and how to appropriate it.

3. Requesting with vain repetition

Jesus said, "When you are praying, do not use meaningless repetition, as the Gentiles do, for they suppose

25

that they will be heard for their many words. Therefore do not be like them; for your Father knows what you need, before you ask Him" (Matt. 6:7-8, NASB*).

Jesus wasn't forbidding all repetitious prayer. He was exposing the error of meaningless repetition and the misconception that repetition itself is the key to effective prayer. God responds to righteous prayers, not meaningless prayers (James 5:16).

C. The Mode of Prayer

There is no specific correct mode or kind of prayer. In fact, Paul said we should be "praying always with all prayer and supplication in the Spirit" (Eph. 6:18). That includes any kind of prayer, on any subject, and at any time of day or night.

D. The Posture for Prayer

There is not one correct position for prayer. I grew up in a rather provincial church that taught us to fold our hands, close our eyes, and bow our heads when we pray. Those are helpful things to do (especially for children) to avoid being distracted while praying. But they're not mandated in Scripture.

In my seminary days I sang in a quartet that traveled around the country singing and preaching at various churches. The first time I traveled with them we had a prayer meeting in the car, and the driver prayed with his eyes open. Obviously that was necessary, but I wondered if the Lord really heard his prayers. I have since learned that praying with one's eyes open is not only acceptable, but it is how Jesus prayed on occasion (John 17:1).

Other acceptable positions for prayer include lifting up one's hands (Neh. 8:6), standing (Mark 11:25), kneeling (Acts 20:36), bowing down (Neh. 8:6), and lying down (Matt. 26:39). The issue isn't the position of your body but the condition of your heart.

*New American Standard Bible.

E. The Effects of Prayer

1. It activates God's power

    Somehow God harmonizes our prayers with His sovereign will and responds in a way that meshes the two together (James 5:16).

2. It aligns us with God's will

    We are instructed in Ephesians 6:18 to pray "in the Spirit." That means we pray according to the Spirit's will and according to His prompting in our hearts. It is the same as praying in God's will (1 John 5:14). When we pray like that, we are aligning our will with His.

    The story is told of a young preacher watching an old sculptor who was on his knees putting the finishing touches on a beautiful statue. The preacher commented, "I wish I could deal such changing blows to the hearts of men." "You can," replied the wise sculptor, "if you will work as I am working—on your knees."

    Prayer can do what no sermon can do. I see the difference in my own ministry when I am faithful to pray and when others pray for me. Every believer can see the effects of prayer on his life.

Lesson

Effective prayer requires understanding its necessity, conditions, content, and hindrances.

I. THE NECESSITY OF PRAYER

A. It Is Commanded

1. We are to be watchful

    Our ability to withstand temptation is directly related to our prayers.

27

Jesus said, "Men ought always to pray, and not to faint" (Luke 18:1). The Greek word translated "faint" means "to give in to evil, to become weary, to lose heart, to turn coward. . . . Real courage requires that we leave the problem with God" (Fritz Rienecker and Cleon Rogers, *A Linguistic Key to the Greek New Testament* [Grand Rapids: Zondervan, 1980], p. 194).

Jesus said to Peter, "Watch and pray, that ye enter not into temptation; the spirit indeed is willing, but the flesh is weak" (Matt. 26:41). Peter failed to pray and shortly afterward yielded to temptation, choosing to protect himself by denying His Lord.

2. We are to be faithful

    a) An explanation

    Paul instructed us to be "praying always" (Eph. 6:18) and to "pray without ceasing" (1 Thess. 5:17). As a child I used to wonder how anyone could pray without ceasing. I pictured Christians walking around with hands folded, heads bowed, and eyes closed, bumping into everything! That would be like the "bruised and bleeding" Pharisees of Jesus' day, who according to the Talmud believed it was a sin to look at a woman, and closed their eyes whenever they passed one in public (*Sotah* 22*b*). Although they avoided women that way, they didn't always avoid walls and other obstacles.

    "Praying always" simply means an attitude of God-consciousness—seeing every experience of life in relation to God. For example, you might see a beautiful sunrise, hug a small child, or receive a phone call from a close friend and react by expressing thanks to the Lord. You realize that all good things come from Him (James 1:17). When you face a problem or witness an accident, you ask the Lord to help in that situation. You see God as an intimate participant in every aspect of life.

b) An illustration

Imagine spending an entire work day with your best friend at your side. You would probably acknowledge his presence by introducing him to your friends or business associates and talking to him about the various activities of the day.

But imagine how your friend would feel if you never talked to him or acknowledged his presence. That's how we treat the Lord when we fail to pray. If we communicated with our friends as infrequently as some of us communicate with the Lord, our friends might disappear.

B. It Glorifies God

God is glorified through answered prayer because it brings Him praise. Jesus said, "Whatever ye shall ask in my name, that will I do, that the Father may be glorified in the Son" (John 14:13).

C. It Brings Blessing

When Scripture speaks of man's being blessed, it is always in connection with the reception of some spiritual or material benefit. God's blessing produces a sense of joy in knowing that God is at work on our behalf.

Prayer can make us happy because it gives us the enormous privilege of talking to God and then seeing His power, love, wisdom, and mercy on display when He answers our prayers.

D. It Brings Results

1. The fact of its results

   a) James 5:16—"The effectual, fervent prayer of a righteous man availeth much." Somehow prayer activates God. He doesn't always say yes to our prayers, but He does always answer.

b) 1 John 5:14-15—"This is the confidence which we have before Him, that, if we ask anything according to His will, He hears us. And if we know that He hears us in whatever we ask, we know that we have the requests which we have asked from Him" (NASB).

2. The timing of its results

   a) Sometimes they're immediate

   Sometimes we're amazed at how quickly God answers our prayers. Isaiah 65:24 says of those in the future millennial kingdom, "It shall come to pass that before they call I will answer. And while they are yet speaking, I will hear." One of Daniel's prayers was answered before he had even finished praying! (Dan. 9:21-23). God may similarly choose to answer our prayers immediately.

   b) Sometimes they're delayed

   Sometimes we must wait for an answer to a prayer because God's timing is different from ours. Jesus said, "Will not God bring about justice for his chosen ones, who cry out to him day and night? Will he keep putting them off? I tell you, he will see that they get justice, and quickly" (Luke 18:7-8, NIV*). Believers may have to endure suffering, but God will eventually answer their prayers.

3. The nature of its results

   a) Sometimes they're different from what we request

   Paul said, "To keep me from exalting myself, there was given me a thorn in the flesh, a messenger of Satan to buffet me. . . . Concerning this I entreated the Lord three times that it might depart from me. And He has said to me, 'My grace is sufficient for you, for power is perfected in weakness'" (2 Cor. 12:7-9, NASB).

*New International Version.

30

That wasn't the answer Paul wanted, but he was content with it because he trusted God's judgment and was committed to obeying His will (cf. v. 10). That should be our attitude as well.

b) Sometimes they're greater than we request

(1) Jeremiah 33:3—The Lord said, "Call unto me, and I will answer thee, and show thee great and mighty things, which thou knowest not."

(2) Ephesians 3:20—"Now unto him who is able to do exceeding abundantly above all that we can ask or think, according to the power that worketh in us."

II. THE CONDITIONS OF PRAYER

A. Praying in Jesus' Name

Jesus said, "Whatever ye shall ask in my name, that will I do, that the Father may be glorified in the Son. If ye shall ask anything in my name, I will do it" (John 14:13-14).

1. Explained

a) What it doesn't mean

Some Christians wrongly think that praying in Jesus' name is simply adding the formula "In Jesus' name, Amen" to the end of a prayer. Some even believe that God won't hear prayers that don't end that way. One man said that such prayers are like sending letters to God without stamps. But the prayers recorded in the New Testament don't support that view (cf. Matt. 6:9-13).

b) What it does mean

The name of Jesus speaks of all that He is. Therefore, to pray in the name of Jesus is to pray "according to his will and instruction, in order that the [great] commission may be fulfilled. . . . This is the reason why [our] prayers are heard" (Hans Bietenhard, "Name,"

31

in *The New International Dictionary of New Testament Theology,* edited by Colin Brown, vol. 2 [Grand Rapids: Zondervan], p. 654).

2. Illustrated

   Peter said to a lame man, "In the name of Jesus Christ of Nazareth, rise up and walk" (Acts 3:6). He didn't use Christ's name as a magical formula by which the man would be healed. Rather, it was because of who Christ is that the man was healed.

3. Applied

   Try praying this way: "Father, I know that everything I've requested from You is exactly what Jesus would want." That will not only purge selfish motives and requests, but will also serve as a practical reminder of what it means to pray in Jesus' name.

Do You Pray Selfishly?

One night a little boy knelt beside his bed and prayed, "God bless Mommy and Daddy." Then at the top of his voice he said, "And God, I'd like a new bicycle!" His somewhat startled dad said, "Johnny, God isn't deaf!" Johnny replied, "I know. But Grandma's in the next room, and she's hard of hearing."

Like Johnny, sometimes our motives in prayer aren't what they should be. James 4:3 says, "You ask and do not receive, because you ask with wrong motives, so that you may spend it on your pleasures" (NASB). Wrong motives can lead to prayers that receive a negative answer from God. But He always hears and answers prayers that are consistent with His will and are prayed with pure hearts.

When you pray, do you have His will and His glory in mind? Would Jesus approve of the things you request? That's what it means to pray unselfishly in His name.

B. Praying in Faith

God wants us to believe in Him and trust Him to respond to our prayers. After cursing a fig tree, Jesus said to His disciples, "Verily I say unto you, If ye have faith, and doubt not, ye shall not only do this which is done to the fig tree, but also, if ye shall say unto this mountain, Be thou removed, and be thou cast into the sea, it shall be done. And all things, whatever ye shall ask in prayer, believing, ye shall receive" (Matt. 21:21-22).

An elderly lady moved to a piece of property that had a huge mound of dirt in the backyard on the spot where she wanted to plant a garden. One night after reading that faith could move mountains, she decided to ask God to remove the mound of dirt from her yard. Before going to bed, she knelt and prayed, "O Lord, I know You can remove mountains, and I believe You will remove mine." The next morning when she looked out the window, the dirt was still there. "Aha," she said, "I knew it!" She didn't really believe God would answer her prayer.

C. Praying in God's Will

First John 5:14-15 says, "This is the confidence that we have in him, that, if we ask any thing according to His will, He heareth us; and if we know that he hear us, whatever we ask, we know that we have the petitions that we desired of him." God doesn't whimsically respond to everything we ask for. We must learn about His will from His Word and pray consistently with what He wants to accomplish.

D. Praying from a Pure Heart

James said, "The effectual, fervent prayer of a *righteous* man availeth much" (James 5:16, emphasis added). If you have unconfessed sin in your life, the channel of prayer is closed off. Psalm 66:18 says, "If I regard iniquity in my heart, the Lord will not hear me."

E. Praying with Earnestness

God wants our prayers to reflect our dependence on Him. Jesus said to His disciples, "Suppose one of you shall have a friend, and shall go to him at midnight, and say to him, 'Friend, lend me three loaves; for a friend of mine has come to me from a journey, and I have nothing to set before him'; and from inside he shall answer and say, 'Do not bother me; the door has already been shut and my children and I are in bed; I cannot get up and give you anything.'

"I tell you, even though he will not get up and give him anything because he is his friend, yet because of his persistence he will get up and give him as much as he needs. And I say to you, ask, and it shall be given to you; seek, and you shall find; knock, and it shall be opened to you. For everyone who asks, receives; and he who seeks, finds; and to him who knocks, it shall be opened" (Luke 11:5-10, NASB).

That doesn't support endless or meaningless repetition in our prayers. It is an analogy for seeking God's will with intensity and desire.

III. THE CONTENT OF PRAYER

Ephesians 6:18 says, "Praying always with all prayer and supplication in the Spirit." "All prayer" speaks of various kinds of prayer: standing, sitting, crying out, whispering, interceding [praying for others], or making supplication [requesting things] in private or in public.

The Bible tells us we're to pray for ourselves (cf. Phil. 4:6-7) and for others (cf. Matt. 9:37-38; 1 Tim. 2:1-4, 8). Regarding others, the Bible gives us specific requests to pray, such as asking the Lord to send laborers into His harvest (missionaries, teachers, and preachers; Luke 10:2) and praying for those in authority (political leaders and law enforcement personnel; 1 Tim. 2:1-2). Do you pray for those people?

IV. THE HINDRANCES TO PRAYER

Generally speaking, sin is the main hindrance to prayer: "If I regard iniquity in my heart, the Lord will not hear me" (Ps. 66:18). Sin can take many forms, including:

A. Selfishness

   James 4:3 says, "You ask and do not receive, because you ask with wrong motives, so that you may spend it on your pleasures" (NASB).

B. Marital Problems

   Peter said, "You husbands . . . live with your wives in an understanding way . . . and grant her honor as a fellow heir of the grace of life, so that your prayers may not be hindered" (1 Pet. 3:7, NASB).

C. Doubt

   James 1:5-8 says, "If any of you lacks wisdom, let him ask of God . . . in faith without any doubting, for the one who doubts is like the surf of the sea driven and tossed by the wind. For let not that man expect that he will receive anything from the Lord, being a double-minded man, unstable in all his ways" (NASB).

D. Lack of Concern

   Proverbs 21:13 says, "He who shuts his ear to the cry of the poor will also cry himself and not be answered" (NASB). "Only the merciful find mercy [Matt. 5:7]; the unmerciful rich man, who has no ear for the cry . . . of him who is without support and means of subsistence . . . will also remain unheard when he himself, in the time of need, calls upon God for help" (Franz Delitzsch, *Biblical Commentary on the Proverbs of Solomon* [Grand Rapids: Eerdmans, 1984 reprint], p. 72).

E. Lack of Forgiveness

Jesus said, "Whenever you stand praying, forgive, if you have anything against anyone; so that your Father also who is in heaven may forgive you your transgressions" (Mark 11:25, NASB).

F. Idolatry

In Ezekiel 14:3 the Lord says, "Son of man, [the elders of Israel] have set up their idols in their hearts, and have put right before their faces the stumbling block of their iniquity. Should I be consulted by them at all?" (NASB).

Questions and Answers

1. *How can we teach children to pray?*

A good model for children is the Lord's Prayer (Matt. 6:9-13) because it teaches them the basic elements of prayer: God is their Father, He is in heaven, He provides their daily necessities, He forgives their sins, and His kingdom will come.

Another suggestion is to have them share prayer requests with other family members, and then as a family pray for each other's requests.

2. *How should I approach my husband about his use of a repetitious, formalized prayer before family meals?*

At an appropriate time, gently and tactfully ask him if he would be willing to add variety to his prayers to teach the children more about prayer. You might suggest that a different person pray at each meal. In addition to thanking the Lord for the meal, their prayers could include one or two requests—for a school or work situation, or for a friend's illness.

3. *Would you comment on fleeces?*

The idea of determining God's will by establishing conditions comes from Gideon's fleece in Judges 6:36-40. God honored Gideon's conditional request, but that is not how He normally reveals His will. I believe laying such fleeces presume on God's will and timing by trying to force God to do a specific thing in a specific time frame. Don't do that. That's what Satan tried to do when he tempted Jesus (Matt. 4:1-11). The Lord's response was, "You shall not put the Lord your God to the test" (v. 7, NASB).

4. *How can we know God's will when we're faced with choosing between two good options?*

I don't think God wants us to be in limbo, unable to decide which option is His will for us. The Holy Spirit will guide us in making such decisions.

If you're walking by the Spirit, determining God's will on decisions not specifically addressed in Scripture is usually a matter of doing what you desire most to do. I believe that God will direct you through your desires and will eliminate options He doesn't want you to have (cf. Acts 16:7; Rom. 1:9-10).

At such times I think it is usually best to make a choice and then see if God confirms that choice. I usually choose the most difficult option because the greater the challenge, the more demanding it will be and the greater reward it will bring. That also helps me to depend on God's strength.

5. *Should we ever stop praying for a Christian brother or sister who willfully continues in sin?*

No. We should continue to pray until the person repents or until the Lord removes him or her (1 John 5:16).

6. *You said that we shouldn't ask God for that which is already ours in Christ, such as love and peace. But can't we request that those graces be more evident in our Christian experience without denying that we have them positionally?*

Yes, as long as you realize that the issue is appropriating what you already have, not gaining something you don't have. It might be better to pray, "Lord, help me to exercise what You have given to me."

I react negatively to the implication that Christians lack the necessary spiritual resources to live godly lives. We are complete in Christ (Col. 2:10) and have all things pertaining to life and godliness (2 Pet. 1:3). We must learn to appropriate what is already ours.

7. *You mentioned idolatry as one hindrance to prayer. I understand that idols don't necessarily have to be graven images, but will you explain what some of the "idols" in our lives might be?*

An idol is anything in your life that substitutes or takes precedence over God. It might be a boyfriend or girl friend, money, humanism, education, sex, alcohol, a sport, or a hobby. It is anything that dominates your life and diverts you from worshiping and obeying God (cf. 1 Cor. 6:12).

8. *Please explain what it means to say, "If it's Your will," when we pray.*

Praying for God's will to be done is simply acknowledging your willingness to let Him have the final word in your life. It demonstrates your trust in His sovereignty and grace.

If we disregard His will, we might request things we shouldn't have. God might even grant such requests just to teach us a lesson. That happened to Israel when they rejected God as their king and demanded a human king (1 Sam. 8:4-5). God gave them Saul, a disaster of a king.

9. *How can I move God to act through prayer?*

Somehow God's sovereignty and man's will harmonize in prayer. How that works is a mystery, but clearly it happens. In Exodus 32:10-14, for example, God told Moses He was going to destroy Israel, but He spared them when Moses prayed.

10. *In light of what God did to Israel when they asked for a king, how can we know whether we're requesting something God wants us to have?*

One important key is to examine your motives. In Israel's case, they wanted a king because the other nations had kings. They rejected God's rule because they wanted to keep in step with the times. That's not a righteous motive. If your motive is pure, you'll have nothing to fear.

11. *What is the point of prayer if God permits a tragedy to happen to the one you're praying for?*

We must learn to let God say no. That's part of trusting Him. For example, sometimes we pray for the safety of our children, but God still allows them die. That shouldn't destroy our faith in God or discourage us from praying. It should teach us that He is sovereign, and ultimately He makes the decisions.

Even when tragedies occur, prayer is still crucial. It is the means by which God grants us comfort and strength to endure the trial and wisdom to trust His will.

Jesus prayed, "Father, if thou be willing, remove this cup from me; nevertheless, not my will but thine, be done" (Luke 22:42; cf. Matt. 26:39; Mark 14:36). He was submissive to the Father's will even though He knew the enormous pain it would bring. We must also submit to His will.

12. *Please comment on the practice of "pleading the blood of Christ" and "binding Satan."*

Neither of those practices is biblical. In fact, they do nothing more than reduce Christianity to magical formulas that have no effect on Satan at all. The most effective defense we have against Satan and his demons is a holy life.

Regarding Christ's blood: it was shed on our behalf, it has washed away our sins, and it has made us children of God. But nowhere in Scripture are we commanded or instructed to "plead the blood."

In addition, the idea that you can bind Satan because you've said the correct formula is illogical. If you live a holy life, Satan is impotent against you anyway. James 4:7 says, "Resist the devil and he will flee from you."

Incidentally, the binding and loosing described in Matthew 18:18 has nothing to do with the devil. That context deals with church discipline.

13. *Can Satan hear our prayers?*

Only when we pray audibly. The Bible gives no indication that Satan can read our thoughts. He was created as an angel, and angels don't know everything (1 Pet. 1:12).

14. *Does God answer the prayers of unsaved people?*

On occasion God may choose to answer the prayers of unbelievers, but He isn't obligated to do so (Ps. 66:18). The prayer of repentance is the one prayer that He always answers.

Focusing on the Facts

1. Praying is to the spiritual life what _____ is to the physical life (see p. 24).
2. _____ is God's communication to us (see p. 25).
3. List three common abuses of prayer (see pp. 25-26).
4. What prohibition does Jesus give in Matthew 6:7-8 regarding prayer (see pp. 25-26)?
5. "Prayer should always be offered with head bowed and eyes closed." Do you agree or disagree with that statement? Explain (see p. 26).
6. What does it mean to pray "in the Spirit" (Eph. 6:18; see p. 27)?
7. List four reasons that prayer is necessary (see pp. 27-29).
8. Define "faint" as used in Luke 18:1 (see p. 28).
9. What does it mean to "pray without ceasing" (1 Thess. 5:17; see p. 28)?
10. Does God always answer our prayers immediately? Explain (see p. 30).
11. List five conditions of prayer (see pp. 31-34).
12. What does it mean to pray in the name of Jesus (John 14:13-14; see pp. 31-32)?
13. What does it mean to pray according to God's will (1 John 5:14-15; see p. 33)?
14. Identify two groups of people for whom Scripture instructs us to pray (Luke 10:2; 1 Tim. 2:1-2; see p. 34).
15. What is the primary hindrance to prayer (Ps. 66:18; see p. 35)?
16. List six things that can hinder our prayers (see pp. 35-36).

Pondering the Principles

1. We have seen that prayer is communicating with God. It is motivated by an awareness of His presence and grace in our lives. Correspondingly, prayer makes us more aware of those blessings. Prayer keeps our relationship with God fresh and sharpens our understanding of His will. Do you pray every day? If so, you know the joy that intimate communion with the Lord brings. If not, begin to do so today. It does little good to learn more about prayer if it doesn't result in leading you to pray more.

2. Thanksgiving is a key element in prayer. One way to learn thankfulness is to keep a record of your prayer requests and their answers. To do so, you will have to pray for specific things and look for specific answers. Review your list often, and thank God for each answer. And remember, a no is as much a blessing as a yes. God knows what's best for you, so be careful to accept His will in all things.

3. Sometimes the demands of prayer can seem overwhelming because there's so much to pray for. At such times remember that your prayers are a delight to the Lord (Prov. 15:8). Be faithful, knowing that He is well-pleased when you pray.

3
How to Function in the Body

Outline

Introduction
A. The Metaphor of Christ's Body
B. The Members of Christ's Body

Lesson
I. Understanding Our Salvation
   A. We Have Been Reconciled
      1. Reconciliation defined
      2. Reconciliation described
         a) Our condition before salvation
         b) Our condition after salvation
      3. Reconciliation illustrated
   B. We Have Been Transformed
      1. Our life-style before salvation
      2. Our life-style after salvation
   C. We Have Been Regenerated
      1. Regeneration defined
      2. Regeneration described
         a) Our condition before salvation
         b) Our condition after salvation
II. Understanding Our Position in Christ
   A. The Definition of Being in Christ
   B. The Timing of Being in Christ
   C. The Blessings of Being in Christ
III. Understanding Our Spiritual Gifts
   A. The Concept of Spiritual Gifts
   B. The Definition of Spiritual Gifts
   C. The Source of Spiritual Gifts

Introduction

A. The Metaphor of Christ's Body

The Bible uses several metaphors for the church: a flock with Christ as the Shepherd (John 10:14), branches with Christ as the Vine (John 15:5), subjects of a kingdom that Christ rules as the King (John 18:36-37), and children of God the Father (John 1:12). Perhaps the most unique metaphor for the church, however, is a body with Christ as its head (Col. 1:18).

B. The Members of Christ's Body

First Corinthians 12:13-14 says, "By one Spirit were we all baptized into one body, whether we be Jews or Greeks, whether we be bond or free; and have been all made to drink into one Spirit. For the body is not one member, but many."

At the moment of your salvation, the Holy Spirit baptized (or placed) you into the Body of Christ. You became a member of His Body. That's synonymous with becoming a member of Christ's church. You may not have an official membership in a local congregation, but you're a member of the universal Body of Christ.

Lesson

To function properly as members of Christ's Body, we must understand our salvation, position, spiritual gifts, fellowship, and love.

I. UNDERSTANDING OUR SALVATION

A. We Have Been Reconciled

1. Reconciliation defined

   Reconciliation is "the bringing together of two parties that are in dispute; particularly, Christ's bringing God and man together, the result of which is salvation" (Millard J. Erickson, *Concise Dictionary of Christian Theology* [Grand Rapids: Baker, 1986], p. 140).

2. Reconciliation described

   a) Our condition before salvation

   Ephesians 2:11-12 says, "Remember that ye, being in time past Gentiles in the flesh . . . at that time ye were without Christ, being aliens from the commonwealth of Israel, and strangers from the covenants of promise, having no hope, and without God in the world." That's a picture of an unbeliever—he is without Christ, God, or hope.

   b) Our condition after salvation

   Verses 13-16 say, "But now in Christ Jesus ye who once were far off are made near by the blood of Christ. For he is our peace, who hath made both one, and hath broken down the middle wall of partition between us, having abolished in his flesh the enmity, even the law of commandments contained in ordinances, to make in himself of two one new man, so making peace; and that he might reconcile both unto God in one body by the cross, having slain the enmity thereby."

By His atoning death, Christ reconciled not only Jewish and Gentile believers but, more importantly He reconciled God and man. He broke down the sin barrier that separated men from God and men from one another. Now all who are joined to Christ are also united with one another in Him (1 Cor. 6:17).

3. Reconciliation illustrated

The story is told of a World War II battle between French and German troops. The German troops were occupying a French farmhouse, and the French troops were trying to recapture it. As the troops shot at each other across a large field, one of the French soldiers suddenly cried out, "Hold your fire! Hold your fire!"

Somehow a baby had got out of the farmhouse and was crawling across the field in the line of fire. Both sides ceased firing until the baby had been removed from danger. A reporter covering the battle wrote in his article, "A little babe brought momentary peace to a troubled situation."

That's precisely what Jesus Christ did, except His peace is everlasting. He came as a babe to establish peace between sinful men and a holy God, and He accomplished it on the cross.

B. We Have Been Transformed

1. Our life-style before salvation

Ephesians 4:17-19 says, "Walk not as other Gentiles walk, in the vanity of their mind, having the understanding darkened, being alienated from the life of God through the ignorance that is in them, because of the blindness of their heart. Who, being past feeling, have given themselves over unto lasciviousness, to work all uncleanness with greediness."

2. Our life-style after salvation

Verse 20 says, "But ye have not so learned [in] Christ." When we received Christ, a whole new life began. We were transformed by the Spirit (2 Cor. 5:17) and given the spiritual resources to "walk in a manner worthy of the Lord, [and] to please Him in all respects" (Col. 1:10, NASB).

C. We Have Been Regenerated

1. Regeneration defined

"Regeneration is that act of God by which the principle of the new life is implanted in man, and the governing disposition of the soul is made holy" (Louis Berkhof, *Systematic Theology* [Grand Rapids: Eerdmans, 1981], p. 469).

2. Regeneration described

a) Our condition before salvation

(1) Stated

Ephesians 2:1 says, "You hath He made alive, who were dead in trespasses and sins." Before your salvation, you were spiritually dead—unable to respond to God.

(2) Illustrated

The reality of physical death was graphically illustrated to me several years ago. As I sat at my desk, a little boy came running in crying, "Please, come down the street. My mother needs help; my baby sister just died."

I hurried down the street, and when I entered the boy's home, I saw a beautiful little baby being cradled by its mother. She was sobbing uncontrollably as she repeatedly kissed her baby and did everything she could to draw a response from it. But nothing worked because the baby was dead.

The love of a mother for her child is probably the strongest of all human affections, but even that had no effect on the infant because death renders one incapable of response. The same is true of those who are spiritually dead. They can't respond to God. That's why unbelievers live "according to the course of this world, according to the prince of the power of the air, the spirit that now worketh in the sons of disobedience . . . in the lusts of [their] flesh, fulfilling the desires of the flesh and of the mind, and [are] by nature the children of wrath" (Eph. 2:2-3).

b) Our condition after salvation

Ephesians 2:4-5 says, "But God, who is rich in mercy, for His great love with which He loved us, even when we were dead in sins, hath made us alive."

When we were dead in sin, God granted us life in Christ. Spiritual life enables us to be sensitive and obedient to spiritual truth (cf. 1 Cor. 2:14-16). It gives us an awareness of God's presence, a love for His Word, and a desire to commune with Him in prayer.

II. UNDERSTANDING OUR POSITION IN CHRIST

A. The Definition of Being in Christ

To be "in Christ" is to be so closely identified with Christ that God never views you apart from His Son. In a spiritual sense, you have no identity apart from Christ. You are like an unborn child in its mother's womb—it has no existence of its own apart from its mother.

B. The Timing of Being in Christ

Second Timothy 1:9-10 says, "[God] hath saved us, and called us with an holy calling, not according to our works, but according to his own purpose and grace, which was given us in Christ Jesus before the world began, but is now made manifest by the appearing of our Savior, Jesus Christ." God saw us in Christ before the world began.

C. The Blessings of Being in Christ

1. We have received Christ's righteousness (cf. 2 Cor. 5:21).

2. We are forgiven (cf. Col. 1:13-14).

3. We are joint heirs with Christ (cf. Rom. 8:17).

4. We are accepted by God. Ephesians 1:5-6 says He "predestinated us unto the adoption of sons by Jesus Christ to himself, according to the good pleasure of his will, to the praise of the glory of his grace, through which he hath made us accepted in the Beloved."

5. We will inherit the riches of Christ. Paul said, "[I] cease not to give thanks for you, making mention of you in my prayers: that the God of our Lord Jesus Christ, the Father of glory, may give unto you the spirit of wisdom and revelation in the knowledge of him, the eyes of your understanding being enlightened; that ye may know what is the hope of his calling, and what the riches of the glory of his inheritance in the saints, and what is the exceeding greatness of his power toward us who believe, according to the working of his mighty power, which he wrought in Christ, when he raised him from the dead, and set him at his own right hand in the heavenly places" (Eph. 1:16-20).

   Paul prayed we would understand that being in Christ means we inherit the riches, glory, and power that are His.

6. We have eternal security. Ecclesiastes 3:14 says, "I know that, whatsoever God doeth, it shall be forever; nothing can be put to it, nor any thing taken from it; and God doeth it, that men should fear before Him." When God does something, nothing can be added to His work or taken from it. If God saved you, that settles it. Your salvation is total and complete (cf. Rom. 8:38-39).

7. We are complete in Christ. Colossians 2:10 says, "Ye are complete in him." Second Peter 1:3 says that God "hath

given unto us all things that pertain unto life and godliness." We lack nothing.

In normal circumstances, newborns have all the limbs and organs they need to function as human beings. Although they need to grow and mature, all the necessary body parts are in place. They're not like polliwogs, which sprout additional parts until they become fully developed amphibians.

New Christians aren't spiritual polliwogs. They're total Christians from the moment of salvation. All that is needed is time for them to "grow in grace, and in the knowledge of [the] Lord and Savior, Jesus Christ" (2 Pet. 3:18).

a) We have fulfilled God's law

Christ came to fulfill the requirements of God's law (Matt. 5:17). Because we are in Him, God sees us as having fulfilled the law also. That's called positional righteousness. Our position in Christ makes us righteous before God (cf. 2 Cor. 5:21).

b) We must live accordingly

We must learn to live up to who we are in Christ, matching our practice to our position (cf. Rom. 6:11-13).

I have a friend who played football for the Green Bay Packers. He told me that playing under coach Vince Lombardi motivated every man to play above his normal capabilities. They wanted to uphold the dignity and reputation of that team.

It was much the same during the glory days of the New York Yankees baseball team. Putting on a Yankee uniform motivated men to play beyond their normal level.

That's how it should be for Christians. We should desire to live up to our high calling and lofty position in Christ. But sadly, our practice often fails to reflect our

position, so the Holy Spirit must convict us and re-
mind us of who we are and whom we represent.

Our position in Christ is perfect. Even our spiritual
growth doesn't alter it; growth affects our practice,
not our position.

Being in Christ makes us a member of His Body, the
church. Christ is the head of the church (Col. 1:18),
and He rules it through evangelists and pastors and
teachers, who equip believers to minister. When believers minister, the Body of Christ is edified and unbelievers are saved (Eph. 4:11-13). We all have a
crucial role to play in that process.

III. UNDERSTANDING OUR SPIRITUAL GIFTS

A. The Concept of Spiritual Gifts

At the moment of your salvation you were gifted by the
Holy Spirit to minister within the Body of Christ. Each spiritual gift is crucial to the overall health of the Body. That's
why we must be faithful to serve one another. When we
don't, the Body of Christ becomes crippled and its testimony to the world is hindered. But a healthy church will present a strong testimony as the world observes our unity in
the Spirit, diversity of gifts, and mutual ministries.

B. The Definition of Spiritual Gifts

A spiritual gift is a God-given channel through which the
Holy Spirit ministers. It is not a natural human ability such
as piano playing, singing, or writing. Such talents may be
used to express your gift, but they are not spiritual gifts in
themselves. For example, if you have the gift of teaching,
you might express that gift through writing. Or if you have
the gift of exhortation, you might write letters that exhort.

C. The Source of Spiritual Gifts

The Holy Spirit is the source of all spiritual gifts, and He
determines which gifts each believer receives. First Corinthians 12:11 says, "One and the same Spirit works all [spir-
itual gifts], distributing to each one individually just as He

wills" (NASB). You can't seek or earn a particular gift. God gives you the gifts that are within His plan for your life and ministry.

D. The Diversity of Spiritual Gifts

First Corinthians 12:4-6 says, "There are diversities of gifts, but the same Spirit. And there are differences of administrations, but the same Lord. And there are diversities of operations, but it is the same God who worketh all in all." God has given a variety of gifts to His church. Some of them were of a temporary nature; others are permanent.

1. The permanent edifying gifts

   Permanent edifying gifts were given for the ongoing edification of the church.

   a) Prophecy (Rom. 12:6)

   Prophecy is the ability to preach or proclaim God's truth to others for edification, exhortation, and consolation (cf. 1 Cor. 14:3).

   b) Teaching (Rom. 12:7)

   Teaching is the ability to teach the truths of God's Word.

   c) Faith (1 Cor. 12:9)

   Faith is the ability to trust God without doubt or disturbance, regardless of your circumstances.

   d) Wisdom (1 Cor. 12:8)

   Wisdom is the ability to apply spiritual truth to life.

   e) Knowledge (1 Cor. 12:8)

   Knowledge is the ability to understand facts. It is the academic side of biblical truth.

f) Discernment (1 Cor. 12:10)

Discernment is the ability to distinguish truth from error—to discern what is of God and what is satanic deception.

g) Mercy (Rom. 12:8)

Mercy is the ability to manifest Christ's love in acts of kindness.

h) Exhortation (Rom. 12:8)

Exhortation is the ability to encourage, counsel, and comfort others with biblical truth and Christian love.

i) Giving (Rom. 12:8)

Giving is the ability to provide for others who can't meet their own needs. It flows from a decision to commit all earthly possessions to the Lord and to His work.

j) Administration (Rom. 12:8; 1 Cor. 12:28)

Administration is also known as the gift of ruling or government. It is the ability to oversee the church in an orderly fashion. It also includes teaching, instruction, and discipline.

k) Ministry or helps (Rom. 12:7; 1 Cor. 12:28)

Ministry is the ability to serve faithfully behind the scenes, assisting the work of the ministry in practical ways.

2. The temporary sign gifts

The sign gifts were for the apostolic era—to authenticate divine revelation and the messenger through whom it came. When the apostles and prophets passed away, so did the need for such confirmation (cf. Heb. 2:3-4). The

53

Bible itself became the standard by which all supposed revelation would be tested (cf. Jude 3). The sign gifts were never intended for the ongoing edification of the church.

a) Miracles (1 Cor. 12:10, 28)

The gift of miracles was the ability to perform signs, wonders, and mighty deeds.

b) Healing (1 Cor. 12:9, 28, 30)

Healing was the ability to heal the sick.

c) Tongues (1 Cor. 12:10, 28)

Tongues was the ability to declare the wonderful works of God in a known foreign language that the speaker had never learned (Acts. 2:1-11). It served as a sign to unbelievers, especially unbelieving Jewish people (1 Cor. 14:22).

d) Interpretation of tongues (1 Cor. 12:10)

Interpretation of tongues was the ability to translate the foreign language spoken by the person with the gift of tongues so that all those who heard would be edified.

E. The Administration of Spiritual Gifts

First Corinthians 12 says, "There are diversities of gifts . . . and there are differences of administrations" (vv. 4-5). The Greek word translated "administrations" (*diakonion*) speaks of service. There are many gifts and many ways they can be used to serve the Body. For example, a church might have several people with the gift of teaching but only one or two who teach from the pulpit. The others might teach children, new believers' classes, or adult Sunday school classes. It's the same gift with different applications.

F. The Operation of Spiritual Gifts

First Corinthians 12:6 says, "There are diversities of operations, but it is the same God who worketh all in all." The
Greek word translated "operations" (*energeō*) speaks of the
Spirit's work in energizing the gifts He has given us. When
we minister our gifts in the power of the Spirit, His power
flows through us to affect others.

G. The Plurality of Spiritual Gifts

First Peter 4:10 speaks of a special gift that each believer
has received and should use in serving others. I believe it is
a blend of spiritual gifts especially designed by the Spirit to
suit each believer's personality, natural abilities, and God's
design for his life. It's a plurality of gifts in one package. I
liken it to an artist's pallet on which he mixes various colors
until he achieves the precise blend he wants.

H. The Purpose of Spiritual Gifts

All spiritual gifts are designed to edify the church (1 Cor.
14:26). My gifts are not for my benefit, and your gifts are
not for your benefit. We must edify one another "until we
all attain to the unity of the faith, and of the knowledge of
the Son of God, to a mature man, to the measure of the sta-
ture which belongs to the fullness of Christ" (Eph. 4:13,
NASB).

IV. UNDERSTANDING OUR FELLOWSHIP

A. The Definition of Fellowship

Fellowship is an interchange of mutual concern and care
for each other that includes ministering our spiritual gifts.

B. The Responsibilities of Fellowship

Scripture instructs us to minister to one another in many
ways.

1. Confess your faults one to another (James 5:16).

2. Edify one another (1 Thess. 5:11; Rom. 14:19).

3. Bear one another's burdens (Gal. 6:2).

4. Pray for one another (James 5:16).

5. Be kind to one another (Eph. 4:32).

6. Submit to one another (Eph. 5:21).

7. Show hospitality to one another (1 Pet. 4:10).

8. Serve one another (Gal. 5:13; 1 Pet. 4:10).

9. Comfort one another (1 Thess. 4:18; 5:11).

10. Restore one another (Gal. 6:1).

11. Forgive one another (Eph. 4:32; Col. 3:13; 2 Cor. 2:6-8).

12. Admonish one another (Rom. 15:14; Col. 3:16).

13. Teach one another (Col. 3:16).

14. Exhort one another (Heb. 3:13; 10:25).

15. Love one another (Rom. 13:8; 1 Thess. 3:12; 4:9; 1 Pet. 1:22; 1 John 3:11, 23; 4:7, 11).

V. UNDERSTANDING OUR LOVE

Love is the key to effective ministry. Where love exists, there is true humility, which is an essential ingredient in mutual ministries. Pride focuses on self, whereas humility focuses on others.

If pride is hindering your ministry, concentrate on knowing Christ more intimately through prayer and Bible study. The more you understand His power and glory, the more humble you will be. Then you will be able to give yourself to others as Christ gave Himself to you.

Questions and Answers

1. *What is worship, and why do we do it on Sunday?*

   Worship is simply praising God in spirit and in truth (John 4:23). We worship in spirit when we worship from the heart and not merely with external formalities. We worship in truth when our worship is consistent with biblical patterns and principles.

   An excellent way to worship God is to extol His character and works as revealed in Scripture and to acknowledge His gracious works in your own life. You can include Scripture reading, prayer, singing, or even celebrating the Lord's Table. You can worship alone or in a group. The main thing is that your worship flow from a heart of praise.

   Christians worship on Sunday for several reasons.

   - Christ arose on Sunday, so the early church chose that day to celebrate His resurrection.

   - The Old Testament Sabbath day (Saturday) was a day of rest for Israel. The Christian's Sunday is more than a day of rest —it's a day to remember Christ's resurrection.

   - Keeping the Sabbath is the only one of the Ten Commandments that isn't repeated in the New Testament.

   - The New Testament indicates that the early church met for corporate worship on the first day of the week (Sunday). That's the pattern in the book of Acts and the implication in other parts of the New Testament (e.g., 1 Cor. 16:2).

   Although Sunday worship follows the New Testament pattern, nothing is particularly sacred about the day itself. For believers, worship should occur every day.

2. *What is our responsibility when we rebuke a Christian brother and he doesn't repent?*

   If a sinning Christian doesn't repent, Matthew 18:15-18 gives a four-step procedure to follow: go to him alone (v. 15), take two or three witnesses (v. 16), tell the church (v. 17), then treat him as an outsider (v. 18; cf. 2 Thess. 3:14-15). If he should repent at some point in that process, we are to restore him with love (Gal. 6:1). (For a detailed treatment of the process of church discipline, see John MacArthur, *Shepherdology: A Master Plan for Church Leadership* [Panorama City, Calif.: The Master's Fellowship, 1989], pp. 205-16.)

3. *Does the parable of the talents imply that God will take away our spiritual gifts if we don't use them?*

If a Christian fails to exercise his spiritual gift for a long enough period, it could atrophy to the point that he won't be able to use it. But that is only implied in the parable of the talents in a very general sense.

The context of Matthew 25:29 is that those who trust in Christ will gain everything, and those who do not trust in Him will lose everything. The wicked slave in that parable had no faith at all and therefore was not a believer. Consequently he lost whatever blessings he did have.

A true Christian who wastes his abilities, spiritual gifts, and opportunities will have his useless work "burned, [and] he shall suffer loss; but he himself shall be saved, yet as by fire" (1 Cor. 3:15).

4. *Why is it necessary to join a local church?*

Membership in a local assembly of believers is the New Testament pattern, and Hebrews 10:24-25 commands us to follow it so we can encourage one another to "love and . . . good works." Also, we are commanded to submit to the church leaders who are in authority over us (Heb. 13:7, 17). That assumes our involvement in an organized church.

Also, the first local assemblies apparently kept lists of their people. In 1 Timothy 5:9 Paul speaks of a widows' list. And we know from extrabiblical sources that churches often wrote letters of recommendation for members who moved from one geographical area to another and joined another church.

We all need the accountability and mutual ministries that church membership brings to keep us from growing cold in our ministries.

5. *Precisely what is a local assembly, or church?*

Generally speaking, any time Christians get together in a local community it constitutes a church. But an organized church has elders, deacons, teachers, and a congregation. Every Christian is already a member of the Body of Christ and should attach himself to a local assembly for the purpose of ministering to others and being ministered to.

Focusing on the Facts

1. Identify five metaphors that the New Testament uses for the church (see p. 44).
2. When does a believer become a member of the Body of Christ (see p. 44)?
3. What is reconciliation (see p. 45)?
4. According to Ephesians 2:11-16, what was our spiritual condition before salvation? After salvation (see pp. 45-46)?
5. What is regeneration (see p. 47)?
6. Spiritual life enables us to be _____ and _____ to spiritual truth (see p. 48).
7. What does it mean to be "in Christ" (see p. 48)?
8. List seven blessings of being in Christ (see pp. 50-51).
9. Describe how the Body of Christ functions (Eph. 4:11-13; see p. 51).
10. What is a spiritual gift (see p. 51)?
11. Describe eleven permanent edifying gifts (see pp. 52-53).
12. What were the temporary sign gifts, and what was their purpose (see pp. 53-54)?
13. Define "administrations" and "operations" as used in 1 Corinthians 12 (see pp. 54-55).
14. What is the purpose of spiritual gifts (1 Cor. 14:26; see p. 55)?
15. What is Christian fellowship (see p. 55)?
16. What are the responsibilities of fellowship (see pp. 55-56)?
17. _____ is the key to effective ministry. Why (see p. 56)?

Pondering the Principles

1. The book of Ephesians uses the term "in Christ" or its equivalent repeatedly in connection with the blessings that result from our union with Christ. Read Ephesians, listing all the blessings that are yours in Christ. Thank God for each of them and be diligent to live in the light of your exalted position.

2. We have seen that a spiritual gift is a God-given channel through which the Holy Spirit ministers. Since the Spirit gifts every believer, we all are important to the overall health of the Body of Christ. Review the sections on the diversity, administration, and operation of spiritual gifts (pp. 52-55). What are your spiritual gifts? Are you using them faithfully? If not, ask for God's forgiveness and begin to minister today. Remember, your gifts aren't for you—they're for the edification of others.

4
How to Witness

Outline

Introduction
A. The Definition of a Witness
B. The Responsibility of a Witness
C. The Importance of a Witness
D. The Credibility of a Witness
E. The Sacrifice of a Witness

Lesson
I. The Necessity of Witnessing
  A. We Are Commanded to Witness
  B. We Are Competent to Witness
    1. We have the Holy Spirit
    2. We have our testimony
II. The Features of Witnessing
  A. The Corporate Testimony of the Church
    1. Explained
    2. Illustrated
  B. The Testimony of Individual Believers
    1. Our example
    2. Our knowledge of Scripture
    3. Our dependence on the Holy Spirit
III. Some Methods of Witnessing
  A. Prepare Your Testimony
    1. Relate your former dissatisfaction
    2. Explain your conversion
    3. Explain the results of your conversion
    4. Present the gospel
    5. Close with an appeal
  B. Be Familiar with Gospel Literature

Introduction

A. The Definition of a Witness

Years ago I saw an attempted murder and was summoned to appear in court as a witness for the prosecution. After being sworn in, I was instructed to tell the court what I saw, heard, and felt. That's the role of a witness.

Similarly, a Christian witness is someone who tells about his experience with Christ. The apostle John said, "That which was from the beginning, which we have *heard*, which we have *seen* with our eyes, which we have looked upon, and our *hands have handled*, of the Word of Life [Jesus Christ] . . . declare we unto you" (1 John 1:1-3, emphasis added).

You needn't be an astute theologian to witness. You simply need to tell others about Christ—how He loved and saved you and how His Spirit ministers to you through prayer and the Word.

B. The Responsibility of a Witness

The victim of the attempted murder that I witnessed refused to testify against his assailants out of fear for his life. He had obviously witnessed the crime, but his testimony was useless in bringing the criminals to justice. As witnesses of Christ, it is our privilege and responsibility to testify of Him (cf. Matt. 10:32; Rom. 10:9; 2 Tim. 1:8). We must not remain silent.

C. The Importance of a Witness

The New Testament portrays Jesus Christ on trial before the unbelieving world. The Holy Spirit is the defense lawyer (Gk., *paraklētos,* John 16:7-11) who is presenting Jesus as Savior and Lord. The world is attempting to judge and discredit Him. We are the witnesses called to testify on His behalf. We can help or hinder the Spirit's case.

D. The Credibility of a Witness

The credibility of your witness is directly related to your life-style. After preaching at a prison one night, I was approached by an inmate who said, "I really enjoyed your ministry. It's good to see a fellow brother in Christ. I'm in the Lord's work, too." I was puzzled and asked him what he was doing in jail. "Well," he said, "I got five traffic tickets and didn't pay any of them." I reminded him of 1 Peter 2:13-15, which says we are to submit ourselves for the Lord's sake to every human institution as sent by God "for the punishment of evildoers and the praise of those who do right. For such is the will of God, that by doing right [we] may silence the ignorance of foolish men" (NASB).

Then I said, "Do us all a favor. Don't tell anyone you're a Christian. We don't need that kind of publicity." That was blunt, but he understood what I meant. We then had a good talk about the importance of credibility.

E. The Sacrifice of a Witness

To be an effective witness, you must care more about the world's opinion of Jesus than its opinion of you. Otherwise you will be too busy protecting yourself to proclaim Him.

Lesson

I. THE NECESSITY OF WITNESSING

A. We Are Commanded to Witness

1. Matthew 28:19-20—Jesus said, "Go ye . . . and teach all nations, baptizing them in the name of the Father, and of the Son, and of the Holy Spirit, teaching them to observe all things whatsoever I have commanded you; and, lo, I am with you always, even unto the end of the age."

2. Acts 1:8—Jesus said, "Ye shall receive power, after the Holy Spirit is come upon you; and ye shall be witnesses unto me both in Jerusalem, and in all Judaea, and in Samaria, and unto the uttermost part of the earth."

3. 1 Peter 2:9—"Ye are a chosen generation, a royal priesthood, an holy nation, a people of his own, that ye should show forth the praises of him who hath called you out of darkness into his marvelous light."

4. Matthew 5:14-16—"Ye are the light of the world. A city that is set on an hill cannot be hidden. Neither do men light a lamp, and put it under a bushel, but on a lampstand, and it giveth light unto all that are in the house. Let your light so shine before men, that they may see your good works, and glorify your Father, who is in heaven."

B. We Are Competent to Witness

1. We have the Holy Spirit

In a court of law it is the attorney's job to take the testimony of each witness and build a case around it. Portions of the testimony might be irrelevant to the case, but the attorneys select the relevant parts.

Similarly, the Holy Spirit takes your testimony and applies it to the hearts of others. Even if you don't know what to say, can't answer all the questions, or don't remember the appropriate Bible verses, He will use what you say to build His case. Never underestimate the power of the Spirit. You may feel inadequate, but He is infinitely adequate.

2. We have our testimony

Many non-Christians suffer from guilt and inner turmoil. They long for peace, happiness, and meaningful relationships. As Christians, we have all that and more to offer to them because we've received redemption, forgiveness, love, joy, peace, and all the other blessings that accompany salvation.

People may not understand or believe the gospel, but they're often drawn to Christians who reflect Christ's love and peace in their lives. The formerly blind man in John 9 didn't know much theology, but he was sure of one thing: "I was blind, now I see" (v. 25). His simple testimony had a dramatic effect on those around him. It confounded even the unbelieving religious leaders of his day. Such is the power of a personal testimony.

II. THE FEATURES OF WITNESSING

A. The Corporate Testimony of the Church

1. Explained

The corporate testimony of a local church to its community both reflects and affects the testimonies of its individual members.

Author Gene Getz said, "Corporate evangelism is basic to personal evangelism. In the New Testament the functioning body of Christ set the stage for individual witness. This is why Jesus said, 'Love one another' so that 'all men will know that you are My disciples.' This is why Paul said, 'Love your neighbor as yourself' (Rom. 13:9), and why Peter exhorted believers to keep their 'behavior excellent among the Gentiles' (1 Pet. 2:12).

"Personal evangelism takes on unusual significance against the backdrop of a mature body of local believers—Christians who are making an impact in their communities because of their integrity (1 Thess. 4:11-12); their unselfish behavior (Rom. 13:7); their orderly conduct (1 Cor. 10:31-33); their wisdom (Col. 4:6); their diligence (1 Cor. 6:1); their humility (1 Pet. 2:18); and yet, their forthright testimony for Jesus Christ (1 Pet. 3:15).

"It is difficult to witness in isolation. It is often necessary, but God's general plan is that community evangelism be carried out in the context of dynamic Christianity, and vigorous body life.

"United and functioning in all of its parts, the local church can make a powerful impact upon a pagan community. Then it is not so much the extrovertish individuals who are often glamorized as the 'most spiritual' because they witness, but it becomes a ministry of the total body of Christ, in which all share the joy and reward of those who have the privilege of 'drawing the net' for Christ" (*Sharpening the Focus of the Church* [Chicago: Moody, 1974], p. 41).

2. Illustrated

Some time ago a church in our area threw a party at which someone spiked the punch and all the leaders got drunk. One woman leader did a strip tease. That party and the resulting publicity had a profoundly negative effect on the testimony of both the church and its individual members. Similarly, if you worked for the Mafia and attempted to give a speech on morality and honesty in business, you would be laughed to scorn.

I was shocked to hear that a man in our church invited a lawyer friend of his to attend a Sunday morning service, only to have the lawyer say, "I know another attorney who goes to your church, and he's the most crooked lawyer I know. I'd never attend that church!" One man's life-style destroyed the credibility of the entire church in the eyes of that attorney. That bothered me so much that the following Sunday I said whoever that lawyer was, he'd better get his life right or leave.

I suppose every church has people who undermine its testimony, and they must be confronted for the sake of Christ and the testimony of His church. A pure church attracts people and lends credibility to the testimony of its members.

B. The Testimony of Individual Believers

In addition to the corporate testimony of the church, the integrity of an individual's life makes his testimony credible.

1. Our example

   a) Some negative examples

      (1) The scribes and Pharisees

          In Matthew 23:2-3 Jesus says, "The scribes and the Pharisees have seated themselves in the chair of Moses; therefore all that they tell you, do and observe, but do not do according to their deeds; for they say things, and do not do them" (NASB). That's hypocrisy—they were saying one thing but doing another.

      (2) Selective advertising

          Advertisers recognize the need for credibility. That's why they don't employ cancer victims to promote cigarettes or alcoholics to advertise liquor.

      (3) Slothful employees

          If you profess Christ but are sloppy or lazy at your job, you discredit your testimony to your boss and fellow employees. That's why Paul said to do your work as unto the Lord (Col. 3:23).

(4) Dishonest students

> Students who claim to be Christians but cheat on tests damage the cause of Christ. It's better to flunk than to bring ridicule upon Christ.

If you've ever tried to talk to people about Christ only to have them reject the gospel because they had witnessed hypocrisy in some Christians, you know how devastating a negative example can be.

b) Some positive examples

(1) 1 Peter 2:15—"Such is the will of God that by doing right you may silence the ignorance of foolish men" (NASB).

(2) 1 Peter 3:16—"Keep a good conscience so that in the thing in which you are slandered, those who revile your good behavior in Christ may be put to shame" (NASB).

(3) 1 Peter 3:1-2—"Wives, be submissive to your own husbands so that even if any of them are disobedient to the word, they may be won without a word by the behavior of their wives, as they observe your chaste and respectful behavior" (NASB).

> Wives shouldn't attempt to convert their unsaved husbands by preaching at them, placing "repent" signs inside the refrigerator, stamping "Jesus saves" on their beer cans, or using other such tactics. Your strongest testimony is your godly life and respectful attitude.

2. Our knowledge of Scripture

It's important to support your testimony with Scripture so that those you witness to hear a biblical definition of Christianity. Memorize the verses you want to use. Some good ones to start with are:

a) John 3:16—"God so loved the world, that he gave his only begotten Son, that whosoever believeth in him should not perish, but have everlasting life."

b) Romans 3:23—"All have sinned, and come short of the glory of God."

c) Romans 6:23—"The wages of sin is death, but the gift of God is eternal life through Jesus Christ, our Lord."

d) Romans 10:9-10—"If you confess with your mouth Jesus as Lord, and believe in your heart that God raised Him from the dead, you shall be saved; for with the heart man believes, resulting in righteousness, and with the mouth he confesses, resulting in salvation" (NASB).

e) Ephesians 2:8-10—"By grace you have been saved through faith; and that not of yourselves, it is the gift of God; not as a result of works, that no one should boast. For we are His workmanship, created in Christ Jesus for good works, which God prepared beforehand, that we should walk in them" (NASB).

3. Our dependence on the Holy Spirit

a) His part

Only the Spirit can redeem sinful people. Jesus said to Nicodemus, "Unless one is born of water and the Spirit, he cannot enter into the kingdom of God" (John 3:5, NASB).

The Spirit's saving work is threefold.

(1) Illumination

He enables us to accept the Bible as God's Word. First Corinthians 2:14-15 says, "A natural man does not accept the things of the Spirit of God; for they are foolishness to him, and he cannot understand them, because they are spiritually appraised. But he who is spiritual appraises all things" (NASB).

(2) Conviction

Jesus said that the Spirit will convict the world of sin, righteousness, and judgment (John 16:8).

(3) Regeneration

When Paul first preached at Philippi, "Lydia . . . was listening; and the Lord opened her heart to respond to the things spoken by [him]" (Acts 16:14, NASB).

b) Our part

Our responsibility is to take every opportunity to witness so that the Spirit can apply our testimony to that situation. Sometimes people ask me if I'm ever disappointed that more people don't get saved when I preach or teach. My answer is no because I know that's the Spirit's work, not mine. We must be available to Him whenever He wants to use our testimony.

III. SOME METHODS OF WITNESSING

A. Prepare Your Testimony

I recommend you put your testimony in writing so you can think it through and structure it in the clearest, most thoughtful way. Reread it often so that it's always fresh in your mind.

Try structuring it this way:

1. Relate your former dissatisfaction

Begin with your own dissatisfaction with life before you met Christ. Most unbelievers can relate to that because they're dissatisfied, too. In fact, that's a major issue in our society. Advertising seeks to create dissatisfaction by making people think they need more or something different from what they already have. But no matter how many possessions people have, only God can bring lasting satisfaction.

2. Explain your conversion

   Tell of your repentance and how Christ replaced your
   dissatisfaction with His peace and contentment. Use
   Scripture to lay a biblical foundation for your experience.

3. Explain the results of your conversion

   Explain the difference Christ has made in your life—
   how your perspectives and priorities have changed and
   how your current goals differ from those of the past. Be
   truthful and realistic. Remember, God hasn't promised
   us perfect circumstances, but He does give us the grace
   to live for His glory in any circumstance.

4. Present the gospel

   Be clear and concise so people will understand the key
   elements of the gospel: the deity of Christ; the reality of
   sin; the death and resurrection of Christ; and the necessity of faith, repentance, and obedience.

5. Close with an appeal

   Always give people an opportunity to respond to the
   gospel. For example you might ask, "Can you think of
   any reason not to receive Christ right now?" If the person says no, you can guide him through a prayer of repentance and commitment to Christ. If he says yes, ask
   why. His answer will reveal his problem, and perhaps
   you can help him with it.

B. Be Familiar with Gospel Literature

A printed gospel presentation can be a helpful witnessing
tool. Many are available, such as:

- *Have You Considered Life's Most Important Issue?* (Panorama
  City, Calif.: The Master's Fellowship, 1990).

- *The Real Purpose of Life* (Oklahoma City: Max D. Barnett,
  1967).

- *Life's Most Important Question* (Winona Lake, Ind.: BMH, 1975).

- *Four Things God Wants You to Know* (Garland, Tex.: American Tract Society, 1985).

C. Formulate Some Questions

Introducing the gospel into a conversation requires sensitivity and tact. It's helpful to have some questions in mind for that purpose.

1. Sample questions

    a) "I have something to share with you that could make a significant difference in your life. May I do so?"

    b) "Who do you think Jesus Christ is?"

    c) "Have you ever considered the significance of the Bible?"

    d) "If you were to die today and stand before God, what would you say if He asked, 'Why should I let you into My heaven?'"

    e) "Have you come to a place in your spiritual life where you can say for certain that if you were to die today you would go to heaven?"

Are You a Faithful Witness?

If you had a friend who was suffering from a terminal illness but he didn't know it, you would be doing him a great favor to tell him about his illness. Although your news might be hard to accept, it would give him the opportunity to face the truth of his condition and make the necessary preparations.

Similarly, you do people a favor when you tell them about the spiritual disease of sin and its eternal consequences. Whether they repent and accept Christ's forgiveness or not, you have fulfilled your responsibility as a friend and a witness.

Jesus illustrated the urgency of witnessing in the parable of the great supper: "Go out into the highways and hedges, and compel them to come in, that my house may be filled" (Luke 14:23). Paul said, "We beg you on behalf of Christ, be reconciled to God" (2 Cor. 5:20, NASB).

Ask the Lord to give you an opportunity to share the gospel with someone today.

2. Sample conversations

I heard of a conversation in which a pastor asked an airline stewardess what she would do if suddenly the engines failed and their plane crashed into a mountain. Startled, she replied, "Sir, why would you ask a question like that?" "Well," he said, "I just wondered what you would do if suddenly you were standing at the edge of heaven, face to face with God, and He asked you what right you had to enter heaven. What would you say?"

After some thought, the stewardess admitted she didn't know what she would say. "You really ought to think about it," he replied, "because for that to happen to me would be a novelty, but for you it's an occupational hazard." He then led her to Christ.

On another occasion the same pastor met a lady who was telling fortunes at a department store. He asked her if she knew where the Kleenex tissues were. Somewhat surprised by his question, she replied, "Sir, I don't work here; I tell fortunes. You'll have to ask one of the store employees about the Kleenex."

He responded, "How can you know so much about the future since you don't even know where the Kleenex is?"

You can use many approaches. The important thing is to have a few questions in mind to help you direct the conversation toward Christ.

IV. THE FOLLOW-UP TO WITNESSING

Jesus said we are to make disciples of all the nations, teaching them to observe all His commandments (Matt. 28:19-20). Therefore, whenever possible, you should disciple those whom you've led to Christ.

The key elements in a discipling relationship are:

A. Teaching the Word—Set a time to meet each week to teach them truths from Scripture.

B. Focusing on Correct Behavior—Warn them about patterns of behavior that need to be changed. Teach them correct behavior from Scripture. Be sure to do so with a loving attitude.

C. Exemplifying Christ—Set an example of godly living that they can pattern their lives after. Your life must be consistent with your teaching.

D. Dealing with Sin—Confront any sinful choices they make, and encourage them to confess their sin to the Lord.

E. Demonstrating Love—They need to sense your love for them.

F. Referring to Others—If you are unable to disciple someone you've led to Christ, get his name and address. Send him resources to study, such as books and tapes. You can also refer him to Christian organizations that focus on discipleship, such as Campus Crusade for Christ and The Navigators.

Questions and Answers

1. *How should we respond to people who believe only certain parts of the Bible?*

People who stand in judgment of Scripture by arbitrarily selecting what they think is or isn't divine revelation are in fact substituting man's word for God's Word. Scripture claims to be inspired (2 Tim. 3:16; 2 Pet. 1:20-21) and sternly warns against adding to, taking from, or distorting its contents (2 Pet. 3:16; Rev. 22:18-19).

People who deny Scripture and propagate false doctrine are apostates. Second John 10-11 says we are to send them on their way without even bidding them welcome. We must not partake in their evil deeds. If, however, they are open to learning about the inspiration and reliability of the Bible, the following resources will be helpful for them to read:

- Norman Geisler and William Nix, *A General Introduction to the Bible* (Chicago: Moody, 1986).

- John MacArthur, *Is the Bible Reliable?* (Panorama City, Calif.: Word of Grace, 1988).

- John MacArthur, *The Transforming Power of Scripture* (Chicago: Moody, 1989).

- John MacArthur, *You Can Trust the Bible* (Chicago: Moody, 1988).

- Josh McDowell, *Evidence That Demands a Verdict* (San Bernardino: Here's Life Publishers, 1979).

2. *What action would you suggest if I'm witnessing to someone who is drunk or high on drugs?*

I suggest that you go ahead and try talking to the person. Sometimes, even in the midst of such conditions, there is an awareness of the truth. Be sure to follow up by talking to that person again when he is sober.

3. *What about women witnessing to men and vice versa?*

Aquila and Priscilla, who were husband and wife, both explained "the way of God more perfectly" to Apollos (Acts 18:26). Elsewhere in the New Testament, men such as Jesus Himself, the disciples, and Paul witnessed to women. I don't see any problem with witnessing to a member of the opposite sex if God gives you the opportunity and if discretion and accountability are maintained.

4. *What is the best way to admonish people and still be sure the Holy Spirit is doing the work? What part does church discipline play?*

First, admonish them scripturally. The Spirit speaks through the Word. Point out their disobedience by reading the appropriate portions of Scripture to them and admonishing them to repent. The Spirit will use the Word to convict them.

Second, admonish them lovingly. Second Thessalonians 3:15 says, "Admonish him as a brother." Galatians 6:1 says, "If a man is caught in any trespass, you who are spiritual, restore such a one in a spirit of gentleness; each one looking to yourself, lest you too be tempted" (NASB).

If they refuse to change, the process of discipline must begin. That could ultimately lead to a severing of fellowship (Matt. 18:17; 1 Cor. 5:11; 2 Thess. 3:6, 14), but the goal of discipline is restoration, not alienation.

5. *What should you do if the person you're admonishing says he hasn't been convicted by the Holy Spirit and that he won't change until he is?*

The Spirit convicts of sin (John 16:8), but He does so through the Word (Heb. 4:12). Therefore you must show him where in Scripture his behavior is denounced as wrong. He may not fully understand why it's wrong, but he must learn to obey the Word anyway and begin to resist temptation in the strength of the Spirit.

6. *What do you say to someone who's trying too hard to be a friend to worldly people in order to "win them to Christ"?*

Psalm 1:1 says, "Blessed is the man that walketh not in the counsel of the ungodly, nor standeth in the way of sinners, nor sitteth in the seat of the scornful." You should be friendly to unbelievers and not avoid them, but you shouldn't adopt their life-style to try to win them. Remember it is the Spirit who redeems people. Your responsibility is to tell of Christ and give credibility to your witness through godly living.

7. *What should I do if I'm persecuted on the job by my superiors because I'm a Christian?*

First Peter 2:23 says, "While being reviled, [Jesus] did not revile in return; while suffering, He uttered no threats, but kept entrusting Himself to Him who judges righteously" (NASB). Peter also said, "If you are reviled for the name of Christ, you are blessed, because the Spirit of glory and of God rests upon you" (1 Pet. 4:14, NASB). Showing a meek and quiet spirit during persecution brings glory to God (1 Pet. 4:16).

8. *If you're witnessing to an unbeliever, and another Christian who is present contradicts something you say, what should you do?*

Don't ever argue with another Christian over doctrinal issues in front of an unbeliever. You can discuss those issues at a later time. If the issue is crucial to understanding salvation, set a time when you can meet again with the unbeliever to clarify the issue.

9. *One of the keys to witnessing is a thorough knowledge of Scripture, but how much should we study other things, such as current trends in our society, to better understand the perspectives of others?*

I think it is good to read about what's happening in the world so you can understand how people think and perceive various issues. That can be very helpful in a witnessing situation. But the primary thing is to know Scripture so you can introduce God's perspective into a conversation. The Spirit will make the application.

Focusing on the Facts

1. What three aspects of witnessing does John mention in 1 John 1:1 (see p. 62)?
2. The credibility of your witness is directly related to your _____ (see p. 63).
3. What command did Jesus give the disciples in Matthew 28:19-20 (see p. 64)?
4. What analogy does Jesus use in Matthew 5:14-16 to describe believers (see p. 64)?

5. How does the Holy Spirit make Christians competent to witness (see pp. 64-65)?
6. Is your testimony for Christ affected in any way by the corporate testimony of your church? Explain (see pp. 65-67).
7. How does Jesus describe the Jewish religious leaders in Matthew 23:2-3 (see p. 67)?
8. How should a Christian respond when being persecuted for righteousness (1 Pet. 3:16; see p. 68)?
9. What is the best way for a wife to testify to her unsaved husband (1 Pet. 3:1; see p. 68)?
10. Cite some Scriptures you might memorize to help explain the gospel to an unbeliever (see pp. 68-69).
11. Identify five elements of a personal testimony (see pp. 70-71).
12. What are some key elements in a discipling relationship (see p. 74)?

Pondering the Principles

1. It's been rightly said that actions speak louder than words. That's especially true of our testimony for Christ. People are more likely to listen to us if we have integrity. What about you? Is there an attitude or behavior pattern in your life that could undermine your testimony? If so, are you willing to change it? Confess it to the Lord and ask Him to protect you from hypocrisy. Find a Christian brother or sister who will pray with you and hold you accountable for the changes you need to make.

2. We have seen the importance of having a clear, concise testimony. Have you given yours the careful thought it needs? If not, review the suggestions on pages 70-71, and begin to work on it. Then ask the Holy Spirit to give you someone to share it with.

Scripture Index

Topical Index